GOOGLE CLASSROOM

2020 EASY GUIDE

A complete book to google classroom step by step. Learn how to make your online teaching more effective, with also some examples of virtual activities

Table of Contents

INTRODUCTION

Exploring the Google Classroom Benefits

Sharing research with your students in the event of a shutdown is essential for teachers who travel to exams or choose to teach remotely. Most people want to keep our classes as tick during this issue period as much as possible. Some teachers can submit classroom books, but it is challenging to make sure that students do the work they have completed without using VLE (virtual learning environment). Many teachers, particularly those teaching adults, may not use course books and would like to give their students weekly assignments, grammar exercises, videos, and more. Google Classroom will be of assistance!

Google Screen Classroom

The Google Classroom Stream is excellent for keeping up with and engaging with your students. It is a forum that functions. One individual, for example, the instructor, sends a message, and anyone who responds will see their statement below the original message. It's the perfect spot for both job and socialization talks. The teacher will hold text messages and educate us on what is happening. Teachers may also plan messages to provide the students with the requisite details at appropriate times. All that happens in a race will appear on the Classroom Channel.

Student Adding

If you know them, it is easy to add students or more teachers through their email addresses. Otherwise, send the class code (see below) to your students, and they can attach themselves. It would be more fitting for children and young learners to provide them with the class code.

The Position of the Job

Google Classrooms allows teachers to share research with their students by creating jobs, exchanging files or connections, questionnaires, and quizzes for their students. A date can be added to the work to be performed, a score if the teacher chooses to assign an item that makes the student understand the tests and the marks if the teacher uses the scoring facility. When an instructor has allocated the job, the used documents are stored in a folder on Google Drive together. This makes it so easy to copy and reuse every course. When a session is repeated, no student or research is carried out, students will apply their completed work for review, and it will be a new course ready to be re-run.

An instructor can easily use any Google software, forms, papers, slides, etc. when in the classroom. Any tools already created and saved on Google Drive will be available for the courses immediately.

What the students are seeing:

To join the course, students must enter the Google Classroom as a student and provide their course code. It is available alongside the name of the course for an instructor. A small expanded icon is next to it, extending the copying code, etc.

The students go to the Google Classroom, and press 'I'm a student.' They will enter the teacher's class code to see the course. If anyone is registered by email, they will immediately know the direction in which they will be enrolled when joining the Google Classroom.

The stream shows them all that has happened since they signed in last year.

Under your name is an opportunity to display your job, see what you've handed over and what is still excellent.

You should do a job and turn it over. You can add a comment if you like, and the instructor can add a comment even if it is just a receipt.

You may easily add video-links, worksheets, and texts to your students at the most open point. Or, for them, a week by week course can be created. In all things, it's best to start as naturally as possible and forget about the marking system, but when you gain trust, you can do a lot more.

ADVANTAGES OF GOOGLE CLASSROOM

1. Simple to use and easy to access from any device

Even if you're not a regular user of Google, using Google Classroom is one piece of cake. Aside from being provided via the Chrome browser, it can also be used from all laptops, cell phones, and tablets. Teachers may add as many learners as they want. They can create Google Documents to handle assignments and updates, upload YouTube videos, add links, or download files from Google Drive very easily. It will be equally simple for learners to log in, as well as to collect and turn in assignments.

2. Good connectivity and exchange

One of Google Classroom's most significant benefits is Google Docs. These documents are stored online and shared with an infinite number of people, and when you make an announcement or assignment using a Google Doc, your learners can access it directly through their Google Drive, as long as you share it with them.

Besides, in Google Drive files, Google Docs are conveniently stored and customized. In other words, to exchange information, you no longer need emails; you just build a text, exchange it with as many learners as you want, and voila!

3. The assignment cycle speeds up

How about making and distributing an assignment with just a click of a button? And how about learners turning in a matter of seconds their completed tasks? Making and turning in assignments has never been quicker and more effective, because you, as a teacher, can quickly check in Google Classroom who submitted their homework and who is still working on it, and give your feedback instantly.

4. Proper feedback

When it comes to feedback, Google Classroom allows you to offer your online support to your learners quickly. This ensures feedback becomes more prosperous as new reviews and remarks have a more significant impact on the minds of the learners. Google Classroom is a resource designed to help teaching and learning. It is an excellent interactive forum for the students along a course or level that the instructor can customize according to their teaching style and community profile and objectives. There are several ways for teachers to use the Classroom. In essence, it can be used in a teacher-led conventional way or used more creatively in a more contemporary manner, which in effect will lead to more innovation and collaboration among students. There is a diverse range of content available online websites, classes, YouTube videos, forums, etc. that provide tips, strategies, and creative ideas to help teachers use Classroom in creative and inventive ways to match their learner needs.

5. No paper required

There might be a day when it would be impossible to imagine grading papers; Google Classroom is undoubtedly keen to get there as soon as possible.

You have the opportunity to go paperless and avoid thinking about printing, distributing, or even losing the work of your learners by centralizing e-Learning materials in one cloud-based venue! Google Classroom allows students' access to resources, no matter where they are since everything is posted online. Students cannot lose their research in case they have physically lost it in their presence. Since they typically operate on

Google Drive, everything is immediately saved, and excuses are dwindling. Students will encounter more organizational performance with a few short lessons about how to use these online resources properly. Hence, gone are the days of lost worksheets or rubrics. When required, absent students can easily access classroom resources from home – this will also help save teachers and their students a lot of stress in the long term.

6. Clean interface, and user-friendly

Google Classroom invites you while remaining loyal to clean Google layout standards, in an atmosphere where even minute detail about the design is simple, intuitive, and user-friendly. It goes undoubtedly with the saying that users at Google will feel right at home.

7. An excellent device to comment on

For a variety of online courses, the learners may comment on specific locations inside images. Teachers can also create URLs for new comments and use them for further discussion online. This has been shown frequently that technology engages the students. Google Classroom can help students get involved in the learning process and remain active. For example, if teachers have students answering questions in the Classroom, other students will comment on those answers and expand thought for both students.

8. It is for everyone

Educators can also enter Google Classroom as learners, which means Google Classroom can be set up for you and your co-teachers. You may use it for faculty meetings, exchanging knowledge, or professional development.

9. Language and competencies

When the teacher who produces the class or group of students shares content, teachers may take charge of the language levels and keep them related to their learner community, using language at all levels as appropriate. Teachers can slowly develop the learning environment and distribute the course materials at the speed of their classes, depending on the subject requirements and group profile. The choice of which students they are inviting to specific classes enables teachers to delegate work based on the particular learning needs of their students. Teachers can build courses of up to 1000 students and 20 teachers, allowing teaching by a team where appropriate.

10. Content of language learning

A handy feature of Google classroom is that once they've submitted it, it helps students to go through their work. Teachers will get updates about the students' reworks or feedback on something they find difficult. This ensures they can give the students who need it, individual attention, and give them more opportunities to show their learning, operating at the right speed for them. Teachers can easily discern knowledge by determining which students may need extra help, who might want to work with response grids of model responses, etc. The Google Translate plugin for the Classroom is also available to English language teachers.

11. Exposure to an online world

A lot of colleges today expect students to take at least one online class during their degree research. If one gets a Master's degree in education, some of their online coursework might be eligible. Sadly, many of the students never had any online education experience. That's why, at a young age, teachers really should make sure that their students have as much exposure to the online world as possible. Google Classroom is a simple way for students to assist with this change because it's super user-friendly, making it a perfect technology intro.

12. Differentiation

Google Classroom is an ideal resource for differentiation, as teachers can set up several different classrooms. If teachers focus on a topic in the Classroom and have groups that focus on two different levels, they can build two different classes for that subject. This means they can reach out to those who struggle with their kind of job without making them feel bad or dumb.

This can help teachers offer assignments on a more individual basis, and can also really reach out to some students. They can even break people into groups where teachers think they can work the best together. Google Classroom is a perfect, versatile way to make sure every student gets what they need, and as instructors see fit, they can quickly delete and recreate classes.

13. Saves time and cost

Students lose out on all of the 'hidden' costs of studying at an institution by taking online courses with Google Classroom. This includes travel costs (which in some cases are very high), the costs of printing out assignments, and so on, and the stationery and notebook costs.

Although it is difficult to determine how high these costs would be before the students enroll in a course, some important considerations should be pondered over. More specifically, how far a student would drive to an educational institution every day (and how much parking fees if they're commuting by car). If that turns out to be a significant number, they could save money by taking online courses.

Most students find that taking Google classes saves them a lot of time since they work from home-no time is spent on regular commuting. They can even take on a part-time job if they have any spare time, so they can earn while studying. This is perfect for those looking to maintain some kind of stable income while at the same time acquiring additional qualifications through Google Classroom.

GOOGLE CLASSROOM TIES: GOOGLE DRIVE, GOOGLE DOCS, SHEET AND SLIDES, GMAIL AND GOOGLE FORMS TOGETHER TO HELP EDUCATIONAL INSTITUTIONS GO TO A PAPERLESS SYSTEM

Google Drive

Although most of the ordinary users are satisfied with Google Drive based on its storage capacities and file editing utilities, however, there is yet another aspect of Google Drive which adds to its utility and productivity. It is the set of collaborative tools that Google drive entails.

These tools are considered to be best for corporate and academic purposes, which usually need a single document to be shared among multiple users for collaboration and improvement. Google Drive has catered this purpose in the best possible way. One reason for it being the best is the enhanced control which has been provided to the user.

Under this enhanced control, a large set of options is available for the user to specify the sharing abilities.

Google Docs has unique features which in the most basic form for sharing Google documents among multiple users, residing at different geographical destinations. Not only sharing is possible but the collaborative modification is also possible which allows editing the Google Doc in such a way that all other users, with whom the document is shared, can easily see the changes being made in the document.

This enhanced feature increases the competency of work when a single draft needs input from different people, e.g. the corporate files which are based on some program agenda and require input from various departments of the organization.

Sharing of Document over Google Drive

To share a file over Google Drive, you will need to follow the below mentioned essential steps.

First of all, click on the particular document which is intended to be shared.

Next by clicking on the "Share" button a setting panel will appear with the name "Sharing Settings" as shown below:

Sharing Settings:

Now in the space under the title "Link to share" you will copy the URL of the file. This URL will be seen by all those people with whom the original user wants to share the URL. This URL can also be given the Public viewership status because the original document can be made viewable to the people we want. You can thus paste the URL over some websites as well.

Who has access?

The second section of these sharing setting is titled "Who has access". This part relates to two major types of information:

The first part is about the show's settings related to the sharing of the document. This part allows users to choose from three different options:

Public on the web:

This setting option, when selected, will make the document accessible to everyone over the web. So anyone searching for the document with the specific URL will get access to the document. Once found, the document can be modified and altered by anyone who gets its access.

Anyone with the link:

Under this setting, the shared document will not be publicly searchable. But it will be accessible to people to whom the original user will provide the URL of the document. Once accessed, any users can then make alterations in the document.

Private:

This setting allows the user to provide access to the document explicitly. In this case, the explicit users will need a sign in for a viewing and editing the document. This setting is especially useful when the document under consideration is of some essential nature.

If the specific document will be marked under "private" settings, then you will need to specify the explicit users to whom you want to grant the permission for accessing the document.

The next step is to mention the people as collaborators or editors of the document. These mentioned people will be the ones who will have permission to edit the document and make amendments. In this case, the email address for the specific user will be inserted in the collaborator place.

Google Drive allows the addition of a maximum of 200 users as a collaborator for a single document.

Here you will enter the email address of the user to whom you want to make the collaborator. Next, click on "Share and Save". In this case, you can also notify the person about sharing by sending an email. In this case, you need to check the box for the option titled "notify people via email".

If you forget to see this option then you will need to draft a manual email about sharing of the document or have to inform the user in person.

Google Docs

The app's icon also allows you to go straight to Google Docs. You can also get there from inside the Drive by selecting the My Drive button and selecting Google Docs from the dropdown. This cloud-based app makes it easy to create, share, and edit new documents such as stories, scripts, and more. There are also templates for things like resumes, reports, and project proposals.

The opening page gives you access to all of these templates, as well as thumbnails of all the documents that you have created or have been shared with you. Options are available to display only those owned by yourself, buy others, or all, as well as whether to show them in a list or grid view.

They can also be arranged by the person who modified them and when. Finally, if you have many folders, you can click on the folder icon to browse the folders and open up the file of your choice.

Clicking on 'Blank' opens up a blank page and toolbar that is very similar to the one you would find in Microsoft Word.

In the toolbar, you will find standard options to adjust the font size and style, add text effects like underlining and highlighting, adjusting spacing, and text alignment and formatting. There is even an editing tool that will make it easy for your collaborators to see any changes that you may have made.

Clicking on the dropdown arrows to the right brings up some other dropdown menus:

- File – Standard options like creating a new document or opening an existing one. There are also options to print, change the language, download or rename the document, and even publish directly to the internet.

- Edit – Again, standard options like cut, paste, undo, redo.

- View – Simple options like the default view, ruler, equations, and spelling suggestions.

- Insert – This dropdown allows you to insert equations, images, links, charts, drawings, tables, footnotes, special characters, and more. This is also where you go to insert page breaks, page headers, and footers as well as creating a table of contents for your document.

- Format – Options that duplicate the settings in the default toolbar. There are also simple photo editing options like image cropping.

- Tools – Here you will find spell check, word count, voice to text, a dictionary, and more.

- Table – All the options you need to insert and build a table.

- Add-ons – This gives you a link to several third party extensions for calculators, different font designs, and even musical notation.

- Help – Simple ways to report issues and find keyboard shortcuts.

- Comments – The Open Comments button is located to the right, next to the Share button. This isn't a dropdown but rather a button that allows you to view any comments on the document and displays any relevant notifications.

- Share – Button that allows you to share while preventing others from sharing the document.

Tips

By using the 'Share Screen' feature in Hangouts, you can share any open window with collaborators around the world.

Using the Explore option in the Tools menu will help you find websites and images related to your topic to help you flesh out your content with additional sources.

Google Sheets

Sheets, Google's answer to Microsoft's Excel spreadsheet program boasts an interface on its main page that is very similar to Docs. Just as with the word processing program, Sheets displays any existing spreadsheets that have been created and/or shared as well as multiple templates that you can choose from.

These templates are divided into in 'Personal,' 'Work,' 'Project Management', and 'Education' groups and include everything from wedding planners and calendars to invoices and grade books. As before, we'll open up a blank spreadsheet and walk through some of the available features.

Upon opening the app, you will be greeted with the familiar grid view and full-featured toolbar and set of dropdown menus.

The options offered are similar to those in Docs with the exception that there are many more that of course are tailored to creating a spreadsheet. There are options to add and delete rows as well as various calculation tools that will help you manage and understand your personal and business data.

- File – Nothing new here.

- Edit – Standard options plus the ability to delete selected rows and columns.

- View – Allows for the views of formulas, grids, and ranges.

- Insert – Ability to add new rows, columns, functions, and other standard options such as images.

- Format – The format drop-down has standard options for formatting fonts and text. It also boasts options to select different colors for your cells

- Data – This dropdown lets you sort your information, select, and even create filers.

- Tools – Provides things like a script editor, form creation, and a personal dictionary.

- Add-ons – Just as with Docs, this gives you a link to several third-party apps.

- Help – Again, nothing new here.

Tips

By selecting a set of cells and/or columns Sheets will give the user instant summaries of data.

By clicking the 123 icons, and selecting More Formats and More Currencies you can convert your currencies into foreign units.

Google Slide

Google slides have now been renamed to Presentation. It lets you create Presentations (much like Microsoft Office's PowerPoint) with different slides in it. Any presentation that you upload to Drive will be converted to the latest version of the Presentation.

Just as Sheets is Google's answer to Excel, so Slides is Google's answer to PowerPoint. And as Google does so well, they have once again designed the interface to be very like that of Sheets and Docs.

The templates are also broken down into simple Education, Work, and Personal sections. They provide a good starting point for your photo album, case study, science fair project, and much more. Once again, for anyone who has used PowerPoint, the interface will be straightforward to get used to.

Top Toolbar

The quick access toolbar provides essential magnification and undoes tools. There is also a number of other, much more exciting and useful options.

- Plus sign – This button allows you to add a slide and choose a layout from a dropdown menu at the same time.

- Text box – Insert a text box of any size.

- Insert image – This allows you to drag and drop images into place from your hard drive or Google Drive. It is also possible to add images via URL.

- Shapes – Functions to add in any geometric form, arrows, speech bubbles, and mathematical symbols.

- Background – A popup window appears, allowing you to choose the background color image for each slide in your presentation.

- Layout – This dropdown allows you to choose where your main text boxes, headers, and sidebars are located.

- Theme – If you are not interested in ultimately building your presentation from the ground up, you can simply choose a theme which will provide you with a default layout, color, and font so you can get to the important business of building your presentation before the deadline hits. Previews of the different themes are available in the sidebar to the right.

GOOGLE CLASSROOM: THE CLASS GOES DIGITAL

Google has also developed a forum to enhance connections between teachers and students. And has everything you can do in a virtual classroom setting. Google Classroom delivers the following advantages:

1. Creating and gathering student assignments: the platform interweaves Google Files, Drive, and Gmail and helps teachers to build and gather paperless assignments. Teachers in the platform will quickly see who has or has not accomplished the task and give clear input to each pupil in real-time.

2. Improving contact inside the classroom: Teachers will educate students, pose questions and make suggestions for students in real-time, and will enhance connectivity both within and outside the classroom. Google Docs is the first Google Classroom.

These records are kept electronically and can be exchanged with an infinite number of people. You can build an ad or work using Google Doc and your learners can access it using Google Drive.

Google Documents can be conveniently arranged and personalized in Google Drive files. In other terms, you don't need to use your mailbox to exchange details. Only make a folder, share it with your students.

3. Updates You will compose and post updates for all authorized users to use. You may attach ties, videos, and even documents as a kind of mural.

4. Send feedback on the class-directed list, the user is free to submit assessments or tasks, set distribution dates, or adding documents or ties.

5. It is also necessary to submit the same assignment to various groups. In online classes, learners may reflect on photos. You may also build URLs for the most insightful comments and use them to fuel an online conversation.

5. Messages the app enables the production of unique messages for classes of students. This

also requires input from reviews to be submitted directly to the student author. Similarly, in real-time interactions with the teacher.

6. Ease of usage and compatibility on all platforms Even though you're not a Google user, there's nothing better than using Google Classroom. In addition to being able to use it through Chrome, it is compatible with all forms of laptops, cell phones, and tablets.

Google Classroom helps you to connect as many learners as you want to build Web papers. And handle your assignments and updates, upload videos to YouTube, add connections, and download files to Google Drive. Learners should be able to log in, collect, or send assignments quickly.

7. Fast work-sharing and submission method you can build an assignment and deliver it in only a few clicks. Then, in seconds, the learners will give it back to you. Indeed, designing and uploading an assignment with Google Classroom has never been quicker and simpler.

You will see missed tasks, check those that have been sent, and receive instant reviews.

8. Immediate input from Google Classroom offers you the ability to offer online assistance to learners directly. This strengthens the eLearning experience, as an instant statement or suggestion has more effect on the minds of learners.

9. No more paper papers quite long, the study of paper assignments might be part of the past period. Google Classroom is contributing to this aim. By centralizing eLearning tools to one location in the cloud, you no longer have to travel about with a stack of documents. And there is no longer any reason to think about printing, storage, or even the risk of missing service.

10. User-friendly and sleek: In line with Google's basic architecture, Google Classroom welcomes you to an atmosphere where any design element is intuitive, quick, and easy to use. The managing of Google Classroom is therefore quick and fast.

11. Google Classroom is available to both teachers and educators and may even access Google Classroom as guests, empowering them to build a class for themselves and their colleagues. Using it for seminars, knowledge exchange, or career advancement.

12. Affordable and safe Classroom facility is free from ads. In no conditions can student data be used for advertisement purposes. The operation of the classroom is restricted to participants of the college. In addition, students may only be class leaders inside the Google Apps for Education domain of their college.

13. Compile content Using Google Classroom to compile relevant learning resources that students can turn to during the academic year. For starters, add materials such as class syllabus, rules, or lesson guides. In comparison, Google Classroom will even store the majority of the class content.

In this program, student tasks are not placed in the same tab, but in different files. And when it comes to evaluating student performance, the instructor will view it directly and everywhere as long as there is internet connectivity.

14. Make assignments simpler With the Google Classroom app, you no longer need book assignments or homework. You can create assignments quickly by merely providing a

15. title, attaching a summary, and a date.

You can even connect some media, such as images, instructions, to YouTube videos.

15. You don't have to get sick of testing the outcome of the exam even though Google Classroom doesn't have the power to construct quizzes or exams. You will use the Question function to ask students multiple-choice questions, and the answers will be published instantly.

16. Assess homework everywhere Teachers can even review the outcomes of their student homework in Google Classroom, so if there is anything to say, only leave a note in the assignment feedback session. The classroom

would also hold the ratings of every pupil in the school.

17. Centralized data management: For Google School, it's all in one central location. Students may display all their tasks in a single archive, and teachers can save eLearning resources. And the operation for the academic year in the cloud and all grades can be included in the report.

There's no reason to think over missing records or missed tests since they're all processed.

18. Rapid exchange of knowledge online facilitators/teachers and coaches can communicate details and internet tools directly with their pupils. Because of the need to upgrade eLearning courses or submit specific e-mails to each pupil.

19. Everything they need to do is use Google Classroom software.

Distribute connections to educational tools and other eLearning content that will support their pupils. This offers students the ability to provide regular feedback on current classes. They can fully appreciate the content and have exposure to digital devices that will improve their eLearning experience. Google Education, part of the Classroom, lets you delegate and gather assignments, show who hasn't submitted them, reveal them, and create different Drive files for each student or college.

In a manner close to Google+, students will publish material in a sequence that enables them to communicate with classmates. In addition to tasks, teachers can incorporate Drive attachments, notes, Excel spreadsheets, etc. and select how to create a copy automatically for the student as well.

To preserve students' safety, Google does not use the Classroom for marketing purposes, nor does it put advertisements on it.

Stars of having technology in the classroom

1. An assortment of assets

Technology gives heaps of valuable assets to understudies, guardians, and teachers. For instance, if an understudy needs assistance with math schoolwork, a site, for example, Khan Academy gives test issues and instructional exercises that can be useful.

YouTube likewise has numerous instructive channels and recordings that help breathe life into learning. Google gives a few augmented experience field trips for understudies and teachers through Expeditions.

There are different sites, for example, Quizlet that permit understudies to audit material. Understudies can even get customized learning undertakings on locales like Class craft.

With current classroom technology, there's quite often an asset to assist understudies with their coursework, regardless of whether at home or school.

2. Proficiency

Technology makes learning increasingly proficient. These days, participation, evaluations, and conduct referrals are often made on the web and immediately shared among understudies and their teachers and guardians.

Parent-teacher correspondence is additionally a lot simpler with email. If an understudy misses class, assignments are often effectively presented on a class site or Google Classroom.

By utilizing technology to mechanize everyday errands, teachers save more opportunity to chip away at making course materials and giving understudies customized guidance.

3. The groundwork for life in "this present reality"

We are facing a daily reality such that determined by technology in almost every manner possible. If understudies are to prevail past the school, computerized proficiency and tech and frameworks familiarity can give them a significant lift. Rehearsing technology abilities in school isn't constrained to making computerized introductions, drafting messages, and altering recordings.

The significant delicate abilities understudy gain. For example, complex correspondence, joint effort, critical thinking, and flexibility will set them up for life in school. What's more, since these abilities are sought after by bosses, they will take care of well as understudies start their professions.

4. Modern data

Technology permits teachers and understudies to have prompt access to cutting-edge data. Where amendments to printed copy, materials occur over a time of months or even years, updates to online reading material happen in a split second.

Gone are the times of removing articles from a paper to talk about current issues in class — recent developments are presently detailed in numerous online organizations and on multiple respectable news locales. What's more, understudies and teachers can even work together to and fro continuously through email and applications like Slack.

5. Understudies have control

Understudies who to learn increasingly about a subject need can explore it's web-based utilizing Google or other web search tools. A straightforward online pursuit gives numerous dependable assets. If an understudy needs schoolwork help, free instructional exercises and clarifications usually are only a couple of snaps away.

Understudies who are progressed in a theme can decide to discover enhancement exercises and work at a speedier pace. Understudies can choose to team up with one another through applications like Google Docs by sharing a report, or they can use it freely. This opens up a lot of chances for individualized learning to flourish in the classroom.

6. Financially savvy

Utilizing technology can set aside locale and teachers' cash because of the entirety of the free, quality assets that you can discover on the web. Advanced assets can likewise enable an area to decrease printing and paper costs. Strategies like mailing report cards to understudies' homes can be a relic of times gone by, as guardians can without much of a stretch check grades web-based (sparing paper, time, and postage). Online course books can help dispose of some rebinding expenses and capacity issues.

7. Propelling and locks in

Technology is entertaining! Understudies are increasingly inspired to learn if they are getting a charge out of the procedure. They are associated with gadgets and appreciate utilizing technology during their time-to-day lives. This degree of commitment continues when technology is offered as a choice in the classroom.

Destinations like Classcraft make learning fun by creating customized learning missions where understudies can travel through experience while gathering data and rehearsing material.

Classcraft additionally has Boss Battles that cause understudies to remain alert while evaluating material.

THINGS YOU CAN DO WITH GOOGLE CLASSROOM

- ## Make Class Announcements

Teachers can publish statements to the stream and send an email to the trainees' Gmail accounts. Students can locate older notices by scrolling down in the stream. The Google Classroom likewise permits trainees to make remarks on the statement.

- ## *Share Resources*

Google Classroom permits instructors to take a file, link, or video and push it out to their students. Using Google Classroom as the constant area for trainees to acquire digital resources takes full advantage of class guideline time. When students are not being directed to several locations to find resources,

The YouTube icon permits the teacher to paste the URL of a YouTube video they currently have found. Additionally, Google Classroom offers a search box to find YouTube videos. The 4th icon permits the instructor to paste the URL of an Internet resource.

- **Keep Multiple Files in an Assignment**

Google Classroom allows for several attachments to a single task. Teachers can appoint the students' multi-phase projects and offer a template for each of the different stages.

- **Develop a Lesson**

The description area of the project allows the teacher to provide instructions to students for finishing the lesson and assignment.

- **Go Paperless**

Google Classroom can produce a copy for each trainee, offering them turn-in buttons for when they are done.

- **Easily View Student Submission**

Google Classroom counts how many trainees have and have not submitted a project. Educators can discover the number of student submissions displayed in the ideal upper side of each project in the stream.

- **Safeguard Privacy**

The documents the trainees submit in Google Classroom are shared just between the student and the instructor. Trainees do not have access to the work of other students. Google Classroom puts all of the students' documents in a single folder in Google Drive;

• Motivate Classroom Collaboration

When creating a project, the teacher can pick whether documents are shared as View Only or that files are shared so students can edit. By selecting "Students can modify the file," all trainees in the class can edit the same document at the same time. This enables every student to contribute to a class project or activity.

• Reduce Cheating

The task folder is available by the teacher only. Considering that the class files are not in a shared folder, the students cannot copy other trainees' work from the folder.

• Produce a Discussion

A Google spreadsheet can be used to gather trainee concepts on a discussion topic. Conversation concerns can be included on a specific page, and extra tabs can be used for multiple problems. When they might have a hard time speaking up in class, this enables for all trainees to have a voice in the discussion even. The spreadsheet discussion likewise permits the trainees to view their schoolmates' concepts to compare and contrast the ideas with their own. Trainee actions can be dragged around the sheet to articulate patterns and distinctions in student viewpoints.

- **Provide Feedback Before Students Submit**

Supplying trainees' feedback while they are working on a task increases trainee inspiration and is more instructive than offering feedback after the job is completed. The instructor shifts from being an evaluator to being a coach or facilitator of learning.

In the instructor's view, Google Classroom produces a project- a particular folder that contains each student's document. While students are creating and editing the project, the instructor can open the assignment folder and insert remarks. The control key and pressing the Enter key will close the remark. Mac users use Command + Enter to close the remark.

- **Email Students**

Sending an email to trainees is accessible through Google Classroom. Educators can email trainees from any task page or go to the trainees' pages to send emails to selected private trainees or all trainees.

• Inform Students Who May Need Help

When seeing the stream in Google Classroom, teachers can see the number of students who have finished the project who have not, by motivating the student to complete the task.

• Project Q&A

When a project is published to Google Classroom, the trainees can discuss it. No longer do trainees need to wait to be gotten in touch with to ask a concern. This extends discovering beyond the class walls and permits trainees to ask questions at any time from any place. When the instructor posts a reaction, it is available to all students.

• Email Feedback

Directly from Google Classroom, the instructor has two alternatives for emailing feedback to trainees. The first alternative is for the instructor to send a global note to the entire class. The second option enables the teacher to send an email to an individual trainee.

• Disperse Notes

Using a Google Doc in Google Classroom enables trainees to concentrate on class activities and conversations rather than note-taking. The teacher can publish the notes from the lesson in the class as an announcement.

- **Trainees Create Google Docs**

When viewing the project submission page, trainees can click "Create," which permits them to begin a new Google Document, Drawing, discussion, or spreadsheet. This file is immediately attached to Google Classroom and titled the very same as the assignment. The document title is added with the trainee name and conserved in the assignment folder in Google Drive.

- **View Assignments**

The instructor's list is split to show tasks "To Review" and projects that are currently "Reviewed." This makes it simple for the instructor to rating and assesses student work. In the trainee view, students can find all the assignments that the teacher has published.

- **Virtual Faculty Meetings.**

Meetings can take up a significant amount of a teacher's busy schedule. Google Classroom makes it possible to minimize the variety of faculty conferences.

- **Streamline Counseling.**

High school therapists can invite all the trainees on their caseload to join Google Classroom.

- **Share Student Samples.**

This provides easy access to trainee work samples. Use the Control key to select several trainee files at once and share them through an announcement.

- **Offer Choices.**

Offering students with options is not just a terrific method to separate direction; however, it also lets students have control in their learning. This leads to increased trainee engagement and inspiration. In the instructions of a Google Classroom assignment, the teacher can provide various choices for trainees to demonstrate that finding out objectives. A recommendation is to label each choice with a name, such as A, B, C, and so on. The teacher can then supply design templates for the various options in the assignment accessories.

Google Classroom shows each trainee's accessories in a nicely arranged list for the instructor to see. Each student can send unique and various artifacts. Teachers can assess trainees' mastery of the learning goal quickly by utilizing the assignment page to see each student's submissions.

- **Creates Folders**

Google Classroom creates folders in Google Drive. As soon as was a cumbersome process in Google Drive is now automatic, what. Each trainee and the teacher will discover a "Classroom" folder on Google Drive. In the "Classroom" folder, the instructor has a folder for each project.

Trainee work can be accessed from Google Classroom or directly from the folders in Google Drive.

- **Connect Directly to Student Work**

When trainees send assignments, their files are offered through a link in Google Classroom. When instructors click on a submission, they are linked straight to the trainees' files without having to search for them in Google Drive.

- **Share with Multiple Classes**

Google Classroom can develop the task in each area if an instructor teaches several areas of the same course.

From the stream, instructors can pick to create an assignment or an announcement. After creating a project title and description, the instructor can set the due date, connect files or links, and can copy the task to multiple class sections. The list of class sections is readily available along the bottom of the assignment or statement in a dropdown menu. Tasks can be copied for up to 10 classes.

- **Show Student Work**

When trainees send work in Google Classroom, their work is conserved in a folder in Google Drive. The instructor can connect files by developing a brand-new statement and clicking the Google Drive alternative. With a student's consent, the teacher can share an announcement with a link to the student's work that is offered in his/her Classroom Google Drive folder.

- **Target Parent Phone Calls**

Google Classroom reveals which trainees did not complete an assignment. By clicking the number above "NOT DONE," the instructor is supplied with a list of students whose assignments have not been sent.

- **Polling**

A task can be developed to find out which trainees are participating in a school event.

- **Share a Document with the Class**

Educators invest a lot of time printing documents, going to the copy maker, passing them out in class, and then waiting on trainees to find documents that they were currently provided.

- **Link to a Website**

Relying on students to type in a web address correctly likewise costs teachers instructional minutes. In Google Classroom, the teacher can offer links to sites. The trainees can click the link and get to the page quickly and rapidly.

- **Peer Feedback**

Trainees can provide feedback to their peers using Google Slides in the Google Classroom. A teacher can develop and share a Google Slides presentation with the students using the "Students can modify the file" permission setting. Each trainee can develop a slide with his/her details. The other students can see their work and insert talk about their classmate's slides to supply feedback.

- **After-Hours Help**

Trainees sometimes have a hard time to complete homework or jobs by themselves after school hours. In Google Classroom, students can publish their questions in the stream to receive a peer or instructor response. Comments or concerns can likewise be included below each assignment or announcement and can be accessed at any time by trainees or teachers.

- **Use the About Page**

One thing that a lot of students will forget to use is the About Page because they don't think that it is all that important for them. But filling out this About Page can be perfect for everyone involved. For the teacher, it is a good idea to fill in the About Page with accurate information to help the student understand what class they are taking and who the teacher is. For example, the teacher may want to consider writing a good description of the particular class as well as links to your website, a little bit about you, and some of your contact information in case a student needs to get ahold of you.

Besides, your students can also go through and fill out an About Page as well. They can tell a little bit about themselves to introduce themselves to the other people in the class, share their interests, and so on. Teachers could choose to make this one of the assignments for the students to be a kind of icebreaker and to help them to learn a bit more about the students.

GETTING STARTED FOR TEACHERS

Google Classroom is an online free platform enabling students as well as teachers to exchange files among themselves freely. Teachers will post homework to finish and rate the pupils, often without needing to print out. This also acts as a way to connect. Teachers are required to post future assignments, announcements, and even contact all students and guardians. It relies significantly on the usage of free based on a cloud file-sharing system named Google Drive. This helps teachers to build and then save assignments using Google Forms, Google Docs, and several other resources provided by Google.

How you can access Google Classroom?

You will have to make sure that you are signed in to Google account before you continue to use Google Classroom. When you do not have one, then you need to create one. You can get access to Google Classroom at the classroom.google.com website. There's even a smartphone version that you can download on all iOS and Android users. The iOS device is friendly to reach your on-the-go school, but you'll have a simpler time to perform things like marking and making assignments on a screen.

To create a class:

The very first thing you will have to do when you activate Google Classroom is to build a class. In the top right corner, press the Plus button, and then pick a Build class. This will pull up a dialog box questioning whether you want to use Google Classroom among students at a school level. If their teachers intend to use it in certain individual classes, Google Classroom allows them to use G Suite regarding Schooling purposes. This offers additional protection and protective safeguards for teachers and pupils. When you use GC for your private use, there's no reason to think about that. You would then have to type the class name. When you are using GC in your school and want to add this material, there's always the opportunity to join a Page, Room, and Subject. Once done, press Build.

Through class code adding students to your class:

The next option to add pupils to your class is to use a code for the class. This is a shortcode that can be used by anyone to take part in the class if you do provide it to them. First, click on the icon named Class Settings present at the top right corner to access it. You can find the code for the class under the heading General. You will post your class code among the students from here, as you wish.

Through email adding students to your class:

You will have to attach your learners to that, once you have built the class. Inviting pupils through email is one way you can do it. To do so, you'll have to move to the tab named People first. Tap the Invite button student's icon. This should pull up a screen where one can enter different email accounts of your pupils. When those have been applied, press Invite. It will give your learners an email, with a connection welcoming everyone to enter the classroom online.

How to use forms with Google Classroom?

Usually, Google Forms were used to build polls, sign-ups, review forms, etc. This can also be used to create quiz questions that you people can conveniently insert into your Google Classroom. You may use many query styles to form quizzes of your own, so they offer a selection of adjustable settings.

How to create a quiz?

You will need to create a simple type of form to create a quiz. Access to the homepage of Google Forms, then press the Space icon. You will need to make several adjustments to the settings of the template before you submit some questions and answers for your exam. In the top right corner press the Settings button. Tap on the tab Quizzes and click on Making this a survey. Turning this on would have multiple questionnaire choices enabling you to select how your students communicate with your study. When you have chosen the settings you want, press Save. Instead, you should call your quiz and start asking questions.

How to view an individual's assignment?

You'll need to switch to the tab named Classwork first to display an assignment. Tap on the submission you want to rate, then press the Assignment screen. It takes the Student work tab for that submission. This is the point where you will be able to display and rate each of the submissions from your students.

How you can add sections to your quiz?

You can divide the quiz into different parts, depend on the number of involved questions. It would allow the queries spread into several sites rather than making these all show on a single tab. To do so, just press on the side, the Add segment button present in the taskbar. These parts may be combined with queries through following very same directions. You may also drag and drop queries into individual pages using a similar icon.

How to select correct answers for your questions?

You'll need to identify the appropriate answers to every query on your questionnaire. Tap Response Key to do so. The panel should light up differently based on the type of query you have picked. Let's look at how to pick the right answers to a variety of common questions:

Just choose the right answers from the given choices using a checkbox or a multiple-type-choice query.

For a question with a short answer, enter the response in the field Attach a correct answer. You may also add several correct responses if the terminology for a given query can differ. When you search Check out the other incorrect responses, any replies that don't fit will be classified as incorrect automatically. When you leave it while not checked, you'll be forced to manually evaluate and rate any responses that are not an exact fit.

Questions in paragraphs don't offer the opportunity to add the right answers. Since they are longer and need further study, each would need to be read separately and evaluated on its own. Choose how many ratings you would want the query to be valued using the Points area after selecting the right answers.

You have the right to use comment suggestions, too. This gives the students input on some issues, based on whether the response is right. Press Add comment feedback and format the responses for right or not correct answers that you would like to see.

When the problem is answered you should display everything and seek to make sure it is right. Only press on the Preview button in the top right corner to do so.

How to add quizzes to classes?

You'll need to submit it to your class after you've done making your test. You will add items, just like you can attach papers, links, and visual recordings to your submissions. Tap the Google Drive button in the bottom-left corner to make an assignment. Locate and pick your generated quiz, then press Add. When you have submitted your assignment with your attached questionnaire, your students should be able to conclude it. Like for every Google Form, you will view answers the very same way you should.

How to do grading and leaving feedback?

You may be required to study and rate these after pupils submit their assignments. Google Classroom offers its page for each assignment, making marking simple and giving reviews to the students.

How to grade assignments from the student work page?

One means of evaluating tasks for students is via the Student Job page. Only click on the grade next to the name of each student, then type in the rating you want to assign. You may then pick them after evaluating the tasks, and press Return to transfer them to the respective students.

Grading assignments with the grading tool:

You can also evaluate an assignment using the tool named as grading found in every single submission. Next, to access it you would need to press on an assignment. You can see a column on the right side of the panel, showing the scoring method. You may type the grade you want to send into the Grade area. You can also give feedback in the Private Comments field for the students. You can click the Return button after you have finished evaluating a submission and are willing to share it with your student.

How to Execute a Pdf Assignment

STEP 1

To begin, you will create the assignment. You can skip the due date on the topic. Now you are going to choose your PDF file from Google Drive, and if you want to choose it from your computer, you can click on the paperclip right there once you choose from Google Drive. Click Add.

STEP 2

Then you will choose "students can" or "make a copy for each student". And lastly, click on assign. All right, so now you will see it there in the stream (let's look at the students' point of view what they will see) click on "show" to show the stream was updated.

STEP 3

Now click on Open. And now, you'll see the PDF file right there. So one thing I want to add is that to do the next step that I'm about to show you, students must have the doc hub app installed in their Chrome browser.

STEP 4

So I've noticed some Chromebooks have had a problem with this too, where you open it, and it should say "open with" up there, but sometimes it just doesn't work. So, what you'll do is right-click it, open it in a new tab. If you do that, the problem is going to be solved. Soon there, you'll see at the top. It will say "open with", sometimes you have to go up and down there, or you open with doc hub.

STEP 5

So what you can do is click on it right here, and you'll be able to type, put your name. You can do a bunch of different things. You can click the Draw tool. You can circle stuff, whatever you want to do. So once students have done that, what they can do is click on the three lines right there, go to download. Then save to G drive. If it says export to G drive on your computer screen when you do this, that's okay. Click export or save, they're both going to work, and click on OK.

STEP 6

Now what you need to do is to go back to the assignment there. Check for the blank assignment. Since you don't want that blank assigned anymore, we're going to exit out of that. Instead, you will click on Add. Go to Google Drive, where it was saved. And then in the top left corner, it should show up, you can see the little circle on there, you will click on it and then add, click on turn-in.

STEP 7

Now it has been submitted. Now, on the teacher's end, you will be able to see it there. If one student has turned it in, just click on it and see. And you'll see the edits that were made on there.

Other Ways Google Classroom Can Help Teachers in the Classroom

Teachers are going to love all of the features that they can use when it comes to using Google Classroom. They can choose to use the Classroom just a little bit or use it to really integrate into the traditional classroom and get so much more out of the whole experience. In this guidebook, we have spent some time talking about a lot of the different things that you can do when you bring Google Classroom into your learning experience. But there is still so much more that you can do. Some of the other neat things that you will be able to do with the help of Google Classroom include:

- Sharing resources: it is easy to share some of the resources that you have through Google Classroom. You can pick to share a link share a video, share documents, and so much more in one location.
- Create a new lesson: you are not stuck with just assigning some work to your students. Google Classroom does make it easier for you to create a whole lesson plan on it. You can build up an assignment with a description as well as with videos, links, and more than one document at a time. This helps to put all of the lessons in one place.
- Make your announcements: if you are worried about your students not being able to find the

information that they need, you can place all of the announcements into your Google Classroom. You can communicate with your students, leave comments, set up assignments and announcements, and more.

- Save on paper; you no longer need to spend so much time worrying about copying pages or making sure that you have extra copies when students lose the assignment It can all be done in one place, saving you some time and a lot of paperwork in the process.

- Make turning in assignments easier: as a teacher you may have come to dread the process of turning in assignments. Some students will make excuses for losing the paper or forgetting about a due date. Some will ask for various copies of the homework assignment. And others just left it at home so it is all going to be late. This can be such a hassle for the teacher to deal with overall. But with the help of Google Classroom, you will be able to put the assignment with all of the instructions online, the due date will be automatically updated to Google Calendar, and your students can even turn it online to save some time.

- Reduce cheating: since all of the documents for the class are not going to be placed into a shared file, there isn't the temptation for students to look through other answers and cheat on their homework.
- Collaboration: the teacher can share documents and then choose if the students re able to view those documents or even make changes to it. Creating a new document and then allowing all of the students in that class to be able to access and edit to it is a great way to set up a group project that everyone can work with together.
- Start a new discussion: starting discussions is a great tool to use inside of Google Classroom. It allows you to hear a bit from everyone, even the students who may not be the best at speaking up when they are in class. You can post a few discussion questions and then ask all of the students to comment and reply a few times for their grade.

- Email the feedback: when you return some of the assignments to the students, you can provide a note that is known as a global note, to all of the students if you notice that there is a common mistake that everyone is making that you would like to fix. Or you can send feedback to individual students if you want to discuss the grade or the assignment with them. Google Classroom offers you the ability to post a note or a comment right to the assignment and the student is even able to comment back if they have a concern or a question. This makes learning a bit more interactive for everyone involved.

- Create new folders: this used to be something that was kind of a cumbersome process through Google Drive, but it is now a process that is going to be done automatically. The teacher will have a folder that helps hold onto each assignment, which makes it easier for all of the students involved.

- Email students. You no longer will need to create a group of email addresses because you will be able to pick out the option to email everyone at once if you would like.

- Find out which students need more help. Google Classroom is a great tool because it is going to let you know the status of assignments from each student. You will be able to go through and see which students have not finished an assignment and then decide from there if you need to provide them with some extra help or not. You can even send out an email notification to these students who seem to be falling behind, offering some tips or some other help so that they can get the assignment done.

- Using the Calendar: this is one of the best features that you are going to enjoy from Google Classroom. You will find that it is really helpful to be able to assign a new assignment and the information is automatically placed on Google Calendar. Students will be able to look at this calendar and see what they have to finish and by when. There are no more excuses for later work or a million questions about when a due date is because Google Classroom will take care of it all for you.

There are so many great features that students and teachers are going to be able to enjoy when it comes to working in Google Classroom. Teachers and students alike are going to be able to get some great results when they choose to use Google Classroom for their needs because it enhances communication, learning, and so much more!

GETTING STARTED FOR STUDENTS

Teachers and educators can get quite a bit out of Google Classroom to organize their students and make their teaching more effective. They are allowed to monitor all of their students in one area, keeping classes separate, making announcements, and doing so much more to help students learn so they can spend more time teaching rather than spending so much time on their regular administrative tasks.

Students can also benefit from Google Classroom. While the students will not be able to add people to the class and are limited on the resources they can upload onto the platform, there are plenty of opportunities for them to interact with each other, communicate with the teacher, and learn in new ways!

Logging In

At the beginning of the school year, your teacher will be able to invite you to join their classroom. You will simply need to give them a preferred email and then accept the invitation and link that they send to you later on. This will allow you access to the classroom, and you can see all the announcements and assignments that the teacher gives for that year. You can also stream content, read materials, take tests and quizzes, partake in discussions, and hand in homework assignments all in one place.

Make sure that the email address you provide is one you use often. Otherwise, you could miss out on some of the important information needed to do well in class. Consider signing up for a Gmail account that is only for school and giving that to each teacher who uses Google Classroom. This allows all your school announcements to be in one place and limits the chance that something gets lost in another email address.

Sharing

Students are allowed to share their thoughts and opinions in the Classroom. Going to the Stream tab, you can provide an answer to discussion questions the teacher posts, and the whole class will be able to see. You can attach supporting documents to this as well including videos, weblinks, files, and documents.

This is separate from where you would do tests or essays and other homework. The Stream tab is a place where others will be able to see your information, what you have posted, and can even comment on it themselves. If you are doing a discussion question or you have found something interesting to share with the whole class, this is the option for you. If you are sending in a homework assignment or a test, you will use Google Forms or Drive to get this done.

Assignments

Your teacher will be able to upload assignments onto Classroom for everyone to see. Rather than printing off papers and expecting a student to remember each assignment from multiple classes each day, Classroom allows the student to get into their class and find all the information needed for the assignment. To see your assignments, you simply need to click on the button to "View All" and see a list of assignments for a particular class. You can see To-Do items, such as if you need to read a document before starting, or a reminder for a test and students have the option to mark whether an assignment is done.

Many assignments will require a link or file to complete. For example, if a student needed to write out an essay or submit answers to a discussion question, they may have written the answers in Word outside of the

Classroom. In these cases, the assignment feature allows students to upload these links. Students can also comment on an assignment, but remember that others in the class will be able to see these comments.

If a student has a question about an assignment, they can simply email the teacher through their Gmail account. The teacher can then respond personally to the student, without notifying the whole class, and get the questions answered promptly.

Organization

The classroom is hooked up to Google Calendar so students can look at their assignments, test dates, and other important information and find out when everything is due at a glance. This can help students to keep track of their assignments and makes it easier to plan out how to get all the work done. In Calendar, students can change the color to match with the class, and they can set up text message alerts to remind them of upcoming due dates on assignments.

Feedback

Google Classroom allows students to discuss various parts of their homework and tests with the teacher. In a regular classroom setting, the student will submit the work, the teacher will grade it with a few comments, and that is the end. There isn't enough time in class for the student to discuss the grade or comment and many may not be able to bring up this discussion later. With Classroom, the student can leave a comment under feedback from the teacher, and a discussion can begin that helps the student understand why they got a certain grade or even clarify their answers. This allows for more discussion and learning than what may go on in the traditional classroom.

Discussion Time

Many teachers like the feature of adding discussion questions inside Classroom. These discussion questions allow students to talk about a particular topic and learn together in a setting that is more comfortable than speaking in the classroom. Sometimes the teacher may not have time for a full discussion in class and other times; this is a tool used to bring shy students out to speak their opinions. Either way, students are learning from each other, considering different ideas, and gaining more knowledge easily.

Google Apps

Google has many great apps to use, and all of them are free. This makes it easy for students to get on and use everything that is needed on the platform. Through Google Classroom, students can enjoy other apps including Google Calendar, Google Spreadsheets, Docs, Presentation, Gmail, Drive, and much more. These are great tools that can help students out at any level of education, even if their class is not using Classroom at the time. Students will become familiar with using these apps on the platform and seeing what a difference they make in learning and presenting themselves.

Other Functions and Benefits of Classroom

There are so many great benefits to students using Google Classroom. While many times the focus is on the teacher and how they will be able to streamline their teaching process and help students learn more, students are getting some of the best benefits out of this tool. They are opening up to new ideas, finding creative ways to learn, and even having more teacher attention than in a traditional classroom. Some of the other benefits that students can enjoy using the Classroom include:

- If a particular lesson is not clear to the student, they can add feedback and save the lesson to a new folder for revisions later once clarification is met.

- Students can privately ask their teacher a question

- The ability to create and also monitor how they are doing in a particular class using Google Sheets.

- Ability to email either individual students or a group of students and start up a conversation. This can be helpful in discussions when missing a day in school, or for a project.

- Students can submit their assignments as attachments in many forms including links, videos, files, and voice clips.

- Reduce how much paper is used in the classroom.

- Fewer missed due dates since they have all their homework in one place and can monitor on Google Calendar at a glance.

- Shy students can reply to questions online and engage without being worried about talking in front of other people. This allows for more engagement out of the class and for everyone to be heard.

- The classroom is flexible, easy to access, and both instructors and students can receive benefits of using it.

- While Classroom is only available for students who attend an educational institution using the platform, all of the Google apps are available to everyone for free, allowing students and individuals to get the benefits of these apps, even if they aren't in class.

- Students can use Google Classroom on their smartphones, making it easier to receive notifications and work on assignments anywhere.

- It is easy for students to work together, even outside of class, and for teachers to provide feedback and comments on assignments so students learn more than ever.

- Better organization—students can keep all the information for one class in one place. This limits how the likelihood of losing an assignment, forgetting about it, or leaving the paper at home. Students can simply log on to their classroom and complete homework assignments, tests, and more in one location.

- Instant feedback—taking tests can be hard, but it is nice to get instant feedback. Your teacher can choose an add-on that provides instant feedback on test scores and some types of homework, allowing you a chance to see how you did right away rather than waiting a week or more for the teacher to have time to grade all the papers.

Google Classroom is a great learning companion for students. There are many great (and free!) apps that students may already know how to use. It facilitates different types of learning, allows even the quietest student in the class to speak up and be heard, and can help provide instant feedback and more discussion between students and teachers to help the student learn more than they can in a traditional classroom.

While teachers may love how Classroom helps them to be more effective at their jobs, students will enjoy how easy it makes the learning process and all the options it opens up in the class.

EXTENSION AND APPS

Extensions are great ways to help improve your ability to use Google Classroom. It makes your experience even better, and this chapter will go over the top ones that you should have in your arsenal.

Send from Gmail

If you want to show off shareable content that you feel is relevant, whether it be for the classroom discussion or research, there is now an extension you can use. By adding Send from Gmail, you'll be able to share the content with others, and it can make sending various things like documents and articles much easier for you.

Share to Classroom

This is an extension made for teachers who want to share web pages to the entire classroom, instantly happening on all students' computers. This is good if you're teaching a lesson, and you want to show it to every student because they won't have to sift through to try to find the web page, and it'll keep them on the right track. It is also used for announcements, assignments, and various web pages you want to share.

You can share it with all the students instantly, but make sure you have it active on all the devices. Students can do this back to teachers too, which is pretty cool. Students can only share this with the teacher though, not everyone, and you can mute notifications for this if you don't want to have them all over your device.

Power Thesaurus

For many students, power thesaurus is a way for students to look up various antonyms or synonyms for anything that they desire. When you have this on you can double click the word from the icon on the toolbar, and then show off what that or any similar or dissimilar words mean. This is perfect if a student or even a teacher wants to beef up their vocabulary.

Save to Google Drive

This is a great way for students doing research projects to save all of their content to Google drive. This saves so much time, especially if you're already working on the other Google tools as well. By enabling this, you can save anything you want, whether it be screenshots, pictures, or even web content, and throw it directly onto the drive itself, to make your life all the easier. It can change your productivity, and pairing it with the other tools can miraculously change it, too.

LastPass

One thing that can be frustrating and annoying for both students and teachers, especially if there is educational software that they use, is the number of passwords they have to remember. With LastPass, you'll be able to manage all your passwords and have them saved. Of course, this does have a couple of privacy concerns, but it works if you're just sick of trying to remember a million different passwords, and want it all managed in a simplified manner.

Google URL Shortener

This is good for teachers who want to share many websites. If you're talking to students and want to link something to them, it can be a bit distracting. This is also a bit annoying if you're a teacher who likes to add links, but they're lines long. With the Google URL shortener, you'll be able to shorten any URL by just clicking it. You can also make some QR codes to send to other students and teachers, and if you're using handouts and want to share the URL, you can do so easily. It's quite a time-saver and makes your life simpler.

G Suite Training

This is a free extension that works wonders for teachers and students, and if you have any question on whether to use this software, it is ultimately the way to go. You can get tutorial videos, interactive training, and even customer support help if you need it. What's more, if you're a student who has issues, don't think this is limited to just teachers, because students can also learn through these videos how to navigate through the Google Classroom software, and from there, be able to accomplish all the tasks that they have on hand. It's quite simple.

Read&Write

This is a great extension if you're casting your screen, and you want to read it out loud. This is also good for students who want to multitask various articles and hear what's being read. This is a great extension that essentially reads out loud what is on there. This is good for those who are ESL or have dyslexia, since it allows them to understand better what they're reading, and it also can be used to help check grammar. It's like digital proofreading for students so that their content sounds good, or if you want to read something, but don't feel like staring at a screen, this is the extension that will help you.

Grammarly

If you're a student or a teacher, who wants to make sure they have their grammar and spelling correct, this is the way to do it. It's a great way to have a second set of eyes on everything, and this is a free chrome extension. Essentially, it revises anything that's typed in and gives you correction suggestions to make it easier. While it may not always be correct, it allows you to have explanations that offer good options to try. It's a great extension to help with student and teacher learning.

Adblock

Ads are annoying. AdBlock is one of those extensions that you should always have. You can get just general AdBlock, but it is also AdBlock for YouTube, which allows you to block all the ads that come from YouTube literally, so you can browse without being distracted. Have you ever wanted to showcase a video, only to find out that it's got ads all over the place that are utterly annoying? Well, you can eliminate that with this extension, and just by downloading it, all of those annoying ads are gone.

Emoji for Chrome

This is a good one if you're going to send lots of messages to other students. Emojis are good to communicate sometimes, even just for an acknowledgment. It's easy if you want to have a way to find, use, and copy different emojis, and it's a good way to communicate with others on the web. After all, a good emoji might be just the right way to communicate with other people's various needs, or even how to respond to various assignments. Even a thumbs-up can be a good acknowledgment.

These extensions will change your ability to use Google Classroom, and for both students and teachers alike, it's a great way to ensure you get the best results and to help make your classroom experience better.

Top Useful Apps for Google Classroom

Do you want some great apps for learning? This chapter will go over a couple of apps that can change your experience with Google Classroom. Read on to find out more.

Math Apps

Here are some math apps that should be included to better your experience:

The first is Motion Math. This is an innovative tool that teaches foundations for math, with some interactive visuals. It can be integrated into your lesson plan. Students can do these problems at their own pace and you just have to make sure they are doing it. It is good for grades K-6, and it can give instructions on how to solve problems with context. It measures the learning of students with a growth mindset and allows visuals to be used to understand math.

Quick Math Pack is a bundle of four different apps that offer some quick learning opportunities for students. These are for grades K-5 as well, and it goes over basic math concepts, fractions, and also telling time. You can have this app bundle for four bucks, and it's great for students who need some extra practice with learning various math concepts. It also comes with handwriting software, allowing the student, to write it onto the interface to remember math concepts better.

Apollonius is a geometry app for students who want to learn basic geometry. It's used to help showcase various constructions that are made with both a compass and a ruler, using these to explore the different kinds of objects that you can make. It is used with touchscreen devices so that you can get the best experience possible with this app. It's good for learning basic shapes too and can help students better understand how angles and lines interact with one another.

Mathspace is a computer-based math system that helps students to get problems fully worked out, and obtain instant feedback and help. It contains over 70,000 different questions, ranging from algebra, and graphing to geometry and statistics. This can be used by students anywhere from grades 6-12, meaning it's a great app for those older students. It's also got math writing recognizing software, where it will recognize the items that are written, and correct them on the spot, providing hands-on help to better your understanding of difficult concepts. This is usually where students tend to fall behind in math, and this software can prevent that from happening.

Assorted VR Apps

VR is super popular these days, to the point where Google Classroom has a couple of apps on it. But here are the best apps to use relating to VR.

Animal flashcards are a great way to use AR with flashcards, allowing children to learn about various animals and also learn their letters easier. It's a unique app, and you get realistically rendered animals to look at. You can tap the image to hear the name or the letters that are in the name of the animal.

The quiver is coloring but made for learning. It's AR coloring, which means that you can color some interesting characters with this technology, view cool animals, play interactive games, and even get quizzes and facts on it. You can learn about many different animals and other factors with this fun app, and it certainly allows you to explore your artistic side as well.

Boulevard is an art teacher's dream. With this, you essentially get the VR and AR experience of going to different museums, to look at the works that are there. Sure, you may not be able to take your class to the British Museum, but this app allows you to explore this experience, and if you're an art teacher who wants to work on art history or even a history teacher that dabbles in art, this is for you.

GOOGLE CLASSROOM TIPS & TRICKS

Both teachers and students can benefit from Google Classroom. It is an easy platform that brings together some best apps that Google has to offer to help teachers get the most out of their lectures and students to learn in new and exciting ways. Here we will look at some of the tips and tricks that both students and teachers can try to get the most out of the Google Classroom platform.

Tips for Teachers

Tip 1: Learn all the ways to give feedback

Your students are going to thrive with as much feedback as you can provide them and Classroom offers you many options for this. You can leave comments on assignments that students hand in, on the file that is submitted, through email, and so much more. Consider the best places to leave feedback and let your students know, so they can be on the lookout for ways to improve.

Some ways that you can utilize comments include:

- Class comments: you can do this by starting a common for the whole class on the outside of the assignment or in the announcement. This is going to be a comment that the whole class is going to see, so don't use it if you just want to talk to the individual student. It is a good option to use if you want to answer a question that a lot of people have.

- Private comments: you can do this by going into the file of an individual student. You will be able to see the submissions this student has made and can click on the comment bar near the bottom. When you add a comment, the student will be the only one who can see it.

- Comments to media: you can do this by clicking on the file that the student submitted to you. Highlight the area and then comment on that particular part of the project. This can help you to show an example of the student or explain your thoughts and how something needs to be changed.

Tip 2: Use the description feature

When creating an assignment, make sure to add a nice long description. This is where you explain what the assignment is all about, how to complete it, and even when the assignment is due. Often students are juggling many classes all at once and by the time they get to the assignment, they have forgotten all the instructions you gave them in class. Or if a student missed class that day, the description can help them understand what they missed. A good description can help to limit emails with questions and can help students get started on the assignment without confusion.

Tip 3: Use Flubaroo

Grading can take up a lot of your time, especially when dealing with many students and multiple classes. You want to provide your students with accurate feedback as quickly as possible, but traditional teaching can make this impossible. Add-ons like Flubaroo can make this easier. When creating a quiz or test, you can use Flubaroo so that when a student submits their answers, the app will check them and provide a score right away. The student can see how well they did on the quiz and where they may need to make some changes.

This kind of add-on is best for things such as multiple choice assignments and tests. It allows the student to see what they understand right away without having to wait for the teacher to correct everything. You can go back and change the grade on a particular assignment if the add-on grades incorrectly, you want to add bonus points, or for some other reason.

If you are creating assignments like discussion posts, opinions, projects, and essays, Flubaroo is not the best option for you. This app is not going to understand how to grade these projects and since each one is more creative and doesn't necessarily have a right or wrong answer, the teacher needs to go in and grade. There are many places where you can provide feedback, even at various points of the project, to help the student make changes before the final grade.

Tip 4: Reuse some of your old posts

At times, you may have an assignment, question, or announcement that is similar to something you have posted before. For example, if you have a weekly reading or discussion assignment that is pretty much the same every week, you will be able to use the reuse option in the Classroom. To do this, just click on the "+" button that is on the right of the screen. You will then be able to select "Reuse post." Pick from a list of options that you already used for the class. If there are any modifications, such as a different due date, you can make those before posting again. When reusing the post, you have the option to create new copies of the attachments that were used in the original posting.

Tip 5: Share your links and resources

There may be times that you find an interesting document, video, or other media that you would like your students to see. Or they may need resources for an upcoming project, and you want to make it easier for them to find. In this case, you should use the announcement feature. This allows all the important documents to be listed right at the top of the classroom rather than potentially getting lost further down in assignments.

This is a great tip to use for items of interest that you would like to share with your students or for documents and files that they will need right away. If you have a resource that the students will need throughout the year, you should place it into the "About" tab to prevent it from getting lost as the year goes on.

Tips for Students

Tip 1: Pick one email for all of your classes

Consider having a dedicated email that is for all of your classes. You don't need to separate it and have an email for each of your classes, but create a new email that will only accept information from all classes using Google Classroom. Whenever a teacher announces they use this platform, you will use this email. This helps you to keep all of your classes in one place and can prevent you from missing out on your announcements and assignments because they got lost in all your emails.

Tip 2: Check your classes daily

As the year goes on, your teacher will probably get into a routine of when they make posts, and you can check the class at that time. But it is still a good idea to stay on top of a class and check it each day. You never know when you may forget about an assignment that is almost due or when the teacher will add an extra announcement for the whole class. If you only check your classes on occasion, you could miss out on a lot of important information along the way. Check-in daily to stay up to date and to get everything in on time.

Tip 3: Look at the calendar

One of the first places you should go when opening up to a class is the Calendar. This is going to list everything important that is coming your way in the next few months (updated as the teacher adds new announcements and assignments) so you can plan out your time. For some students, it is easier to get a grasp on the work when it is in tablet form rather than just looking at a date in the announcements. Use this as a planning tool and check it often to see if there is anything new to add to your schedule.

Tip 4: Ask questions for clarification

The classroom makes it easier for students to ask the questions they need before starting an assignment. In some classrooms, it can be hard to find time to ask a question. When twenty or more students are asking questions at the same time, or the teacher runs out of time and barely gets the assignment out before the next bell, many students may leave the classroom without any clue how to begin on an assignment.

With Classroom, the students can ask any questions they have when it is convenient. If they have a question about an assignment, they can comment on the assignment or send an email. If they have a question about some feedback that is left for a test, discussion, or essay, they can ask it right on the assignment. The classroom has opened up many options for talking to your teacher and getting your questions answered, so don't be shy and sit in the dark when you need clarification.

Tip 5: Learn about all the features of Google

Google has many great features that both students and teachers can take advantage of. Many people don't realize all the different apps that are available on Google, and since these apps can be used together with Classroom and are free, it is important to take advantage of as many as possible. Some of the best Google products that can help with learning include:

- Gmail: Gmail makes it easier for students and teachers to communicate about the class without sharing the information with other students.

- Calendar: students will be able to see at a glance when important assignments, tests, and other information occurs in their class.

- Drive: Drive is a great place to put all assignments, questions, and other documents that are needed to keep up in class. Teachers can place learning materials and assignments inside for the student to see and students can submit their assignments all in one place.

- YouTube: students are used to spending time on YouTube, and teachers can use this to their advantage to find educational videos for their class. Students can either look at links that the teacher provides or search for their videos.

- Docs: this program works similarly to Microsoft Word, but since it is free, it can be nice for those students who don't already have Word at home. Students can write, edit, and make changes just like on regular documents and then submit them back to the teacher.

- Google Earth/Maps: explore the world around us with these two great features. Google Earth lets students learn more about the world by allowing them to look up different areas and see them from an actual satellite. Google Maps can help with Geography around the world or students can even create their Maps with this program.

These are just a few of the different apps available with Google that can make a difference in the way that students learn. While not all of them will apply to every class, a good understanding of each can help the teacher pick the right one for their class and helps the student learn as much as possible.

FAQS ABOUT GOOGLE CLASSROOM

What is Google Classroom?

Google defines Google Classroom as "class activity verification" and this may be the easiest way to evaluate it. This is a platform that integrates Google G Suite tools for students and teachers. Teachers can save course material and share it with students. From this point, you can determine the highlights that you need to put together. This continuous adaptation and integration with the famous Google tools could make Google Classroom the most used Edtech device today.

Google Classroom LMS?

Google Classroom is not an independent classroom management system (CMS), a learning management system (LMS), or a student information system (SIS). As a result, Google usually adds new features to Google Classroom. For example, in June 2019, Google announced that schools would have the opportunity to combine the new assessment overview with the current student database. As Google continues to improve, it may appear and function more like an LMS. However, to date, it is very appropriate for organizations to think of this device as a storage area.

Do you need to register?

All you have to do to use Google Classroom is to log into your Google account simply (Gmail address). If you need to create a new one, open accounts.google.com, click Create an account, select yours, and enter the required information.

Who can use Google Classroom?

Everyone! Google Classroom was created as a free service for anyone with a Google account and free for organizations using G Suite Education or G Suite Charities. In general, students and teachers can access Google classes using the Google account provided by the school. While students and teachers at school are key Google Classroom customers, some features can be used by families, schoolchildren, and administrators.

How do you create a class?

As a teacher, you can now create lessons. To do this, click on the plus icon in the upper right corner and select Create course. Observe options, give a name to the course, enter other information, and choose to Create. Now, look at the course number and the name of the course.

How do I invite students?

Students can sign up for classes using Google Classroom by tapping the + link and then clicking Join instead of creating a class. They will enter the class code and select Join.

As should be clear, the same service must be used for students and teachers so that they can play a role in different contexts.

Can I use my mobile phone?

Google Classroom is available as an application for iPhone/iPad and Android. Download the Google Classroom app from the App Store or Google Play Store.

Can all teachers use it?

If you are a school teacher, you cannot use the free version of Google Classroom. Instead, schools have to offer something called G Suite for education and school boards have to choose this option. The explanatory notes include clear principles on how to manage student information.

How do Google teachers use classes?

Since this is indeed the stage of adaptation, the teacher uses the application differently. With Google Classroom, teachers can:

1. Manage classes. This range includes various Google tools, such as Drive, Docs, and Calendar, so there are many "other approaches" integrated for classroom management activities. For example, if you add a project, it is automatically added to the program that students see.

2. Compile, distribute, and digitize student content, projects, and work. Teachers can launch projects in different classes or modify and reuse them from year to year. If students have normal access to widgets, Google Classroom can help you navigate certain trips to the printer and reduce the need for learning and teaching-related documents.

3. Contact students about their projects. You can use the platform to send notifications and announcements of projects, but it is difficult to see who completes or does not complete their

work. Likewise, you can register individually each student, answer their questions, and provide assistance.

4. Send feedback to students about their assessment and homework. In Google Classroom, you can use Google's forms to create and share exams. You will invest less energy in creating and distributing assessments, but students will receive immediate feedback on their work.

How do I set up Google Classroom?

The basic setup procedure of Google Classroom is completely intuitive, even for novice customers. Google Teacher Center offers some training exercises to help you get started: the best option if you are looking for the latest information and videos. There are numerous video tutorials on YouTube presented by tech and integration experts. Many of the recordings made by these teachers include realistic tips and tricks that they learned while using the class forums.

How can Google Classroom classes be supported?

Google Classroom can help simplify development assessments that play an important role in helping students who may need more help. For example, you can create, collect, and distribute labels or digital rankings with automatic reviews through the platform. In other words, Google Classroom can make it easier and faster to collect regular feedback on student progress. There are many other development assessment tools, many of which are now integrated with Google Classroom.

Likewise, Google Classroom makes it easy to change tasks for individual students or small gatherings. This means that the teacher can assign specific or modified tasks to students or specific groups in the classroom. You also have the opportunity to have a private conversation with a student if they have any questions or need further assistance. The decision to do all this online can explain the experiments performed by individual teachers that are not as important in the classroom as they may be useful to students online.

With or without Google Classroom, differentiation is an ongoing issue around creative problem solving and there is no "right" approach. Fortunately, many teachers share online tips, creative solutions, and styles.

How can parents and families keep in touch with Google classes?

Google Classroom can send student assignments updates to teachers but does not guarantee the extent to which e-mail is detected on devices such as ClassDojo, SeeSaw, or Remind. This does not include drawing attention to direct messages with families or allowing families to comment on their children's work.

What's new in Google class?

This platform has been substantially rebuilt since its release and Google continues to introduce new features. Consumers have long complained about some of its features. Google has fixed and audited this for the 2019-2020 school year. Please note that the administrator or teacher must enter the pilot program for some time to find new integration in the subject and class.

How can I make Google Classroom attractive to students?

To make learning more effective for students, consider introducing the types of resources they share in Google lessons. With G Suite tools like Google slides and

Google Docs, students and teachers can share various media, including photos, YouTube videos, screenshots, and web links. Some teachers even offer students various options for presenting their work in Google lessons. For example, you can offer answers to students by starting projects to show videos, comments, images, and their topics.

If you want to create a smart hub for students, you can do so on the Google Classroom page. In Google classes, Stream is the place where all class participants can find plans and announcements, and it's the most important thing that students see when they enter. Alice Keeler, a prominent blogger with extensive demonstrations in Google lessons, explains the use of Stream to publish her lesson plan and suggests using Screencastify to send video messages to students.

Some teachers include streaming discussion papers in classrooms where students can socialize online, ask questions, or comment on each other's work. This conversation can stimulate interest in the class and give students more value when listening to sounds in the classroom. In conversations, you can use Stream as a kind of closed social network, and this can be a very unusual way to help children use different and sophisticated citizenship skills at the same time.

Which websites and applications integrate Google Classroom?

Currently, many applications and an external page are integrated with Google Classroom. Some of these apps can work with Google, while others can collaborate and share third-party plug-ins in the Chrome Store. If you use Google Classroom extensively, you may have other Edtech tools to simplify the tutorial. For example, suppose students have to learn some vocabulary using Quizlet, you can use Google Classroom integration to share and process Flash memory cards in your class legally. Alternatively, if you are looking for study material online, there is a merger with distributors such as Khan Academy, BrainPop, and Newselat: you will find various articles, comments, and other study material that can be shared with students.

Where can I find more ideas on using Google Classroom?

If you're looking for the original Google Classroom details, check out the Google Twitter tutorial for updates on articles, teacher comments, posts, and even

Google Apps for Education guides. Many fans of the Google Classroom blog, tweet, and share podcast to show how to use the application with students. Together with many teachers and experts in Google Edtech, you can easily get advice and encouragement from other online teachers.

When you use Google Classroom, don't hesitate to find inventions with imaginative technology, tricks, and use of the platform. Like most Edtech tools, Google Classroom is what you create and how it works is truly unique among the classes. The key is to find suitable methods and tools for you and your students in Google Classroom.

CONCLUSION

In the digital classroom era, it is critical that teachers, students, and the people who help them have virtual areas. Google Classroom provides a centralized, user-friendly platform for class communication for all those interested in the learning process.

Google's new education platform is not a digital space for file-sharing or document creation; this is primarily the task of Google Drive and Google Documents. The classroom is not an online space for the meeting; that is Google Hangouts Meeting.

Google Classroom helps teachers to create and exchange projects, quizzes, and advertisements. In its ranking, GUI, class management, and administration can be handled.

Students use intuitive resources to track due dates and upcoming activities, talk with classmates and multiple teachers about topics, and share ideas, material, and thoughts. Parents, guardians, and careers may also be introduced and accessed to reports summarizing the behavior of the pupil.

Google Classroom can be used by children to share art projects, secondary school students who want to retain their education during coronavirus, or by adult learners who wish to have a fully integrated way of managing their classwork online.

ALSO

There are many thousands of persons "Googling" every day with the word "classroom administration." They are also looking for approaches to deal with misconducting students. Ironically, if they invested more time in teaching, they would have fewer students who would feel a need to be disconfirmed. Let's look at what classroom management is and some techniques to make a better environment for your students.

As the term suggests, the way you treat your classroom is all. What processes and protocols you have introduced to ensure your course runs smoothly.

How Students Go Into And Out Of the Classroom

Let's first look at the schedules that everyone at school will obey. When you teach in the first six grades, your students come to school and come to your class. They will also leave and return from recesses, lunch, and maybe some professors. Medium-sized and high school teachers will have students from and from schools, but each time there will be different groups of students.

You need the first step, or your students, to enter and exit the classroom. The classroom protocol must be developed on the first day. Some schools and teachers tend to line up outside the classroom and wait for the classroom. Before your students join the class, greet them at the door on the first day and ready before you ask them to come in. When you're in college, explain why you made them line up for the first time. This is significant! "Because I said so" won't get a positive response and won't give a good initial impression. Suppose you clarify that this is a security issue, whether you want to tell them what to do on their seats or maybe because you want to be able to say hello to each of them when they arrive. If followed by justification, students are more likely to consider a new method.

Next, you should clarify what the method to quit the class is going to be. Can you want everyone to be packed up and wait for rows or classes to be fired on their desks? Otherwise, when the bell rings, will you give the students a final word and let them leave when they are ready? The choice is yours, just explain, explain your reasoning, and be honest with yourself.

Just before the end of the course, the students will discuss what they will do when they next come to study. Check the dismissal process after you do so. You may also want to practice it before the bell rings.

It is essential to develop these two procedures early in the year. If you can start every class promptly because the students have entered the room in an organized way and are ready to work, you will have an excellent time with them.

This is the number one classroom management technique. Have a protocol that everyone knows and can obey to get the students back and forth in the order. Let's look now at procedures and routines to make the time between the bells more effective.

What do students do when they hit their desk first?

After students enter the classroom and go to their seats with minimal noise and disruption, how are you going to start the period? When it's the first time in the morning, it would be like attending and listening to announcements as well as doing homework. Ensure all the students learn how this works. Want to send homework before they go to their desks or allow it to open on their desks so that you can see it when listening to the advertisements? Whatever you choose, make sure that the students learn and can. If you don't have "graduate" assignments, what are your expectations?

What are they to do after you greet every student at the door? On the first day, you will tell them to find a seat and take out their books before the others enter the classroom. When in their chairs, the first-class discusses the hopes. "I expect you to go to your desk immediately when you go to the class and (get your books, put your books off, delete your homework, solve the question in your math books)" whatever you wish to do. You want them to do when they quit the class the next time they come to your class. When you come to class the other time and for a few days and as needed, let them know that you welcome them when they go to college. It does not take long to develop the habit.